An Occult History
of the
Right Side of the Globe

❖

Richard Braden

WAYZGOOSE PRESS

An Occult History of the Right Side of the Globe
Copyright © 2017 by Richard Braden

Edited by Dorothy Zemach.
Book design by DJ Rogers Design.
Published in the United States by Wayzgoose Press.

ISBN-10: 1-938757-32-7
ISBN-13: 978-1-938757-32-7

Dedication

To Patricia
She is the smart one in the family.

Acknowledgements

My personal thanks to Wikipedia. Without them, this text would have been impossible. Thank you, Jimmy Wales and Larry Sanger.

Thank you, David Kertzer, for writing the book *The Pope and Mussolini*.

Thank you, Gavin Menzies, for writing the books *1421* and *1434*.

Thank you, Melanie Benjamin, for writing the book *The Aviator's Wife*.

Richard Braden
10093 Bluffmont Lane
Lone Tree, CO 80124
Rbraden007@gmail.com
303-736-8604

Table of Contents

Introduction

This is a story about two men who have been meeting regularly at the local library in their Midwestern hometown to discuss the issues of the day. They always meet on Thursdays. The man who talks the most is named Giuseppe, and as you can guess, he is of Italian lineage. The second man is George, and he has less to add to the conversation. He mostly asks questions, and listens. He is probably English or American.

Apparently George considers Giuseppe to be the fount of all knowledge. Giuseppe is happy to receive this accolade from his friend, and he spouts off regularly about subjects that he possibly knows nothing about. But he's funny.

The two men know a lot about Europe and Western Asia, so that is what they talk about. They read a lot, but their books are always about the Western side of the globe – Europe and Western Asia. They seem to know nothing about the left side of the globe.

Let's look into their latest discussions.

Chapter One

The Lion Sleeps Tonight

The two men had picked a quiet place in the library, far in the back of the main room, with two leather plush chairs and a bistro table between them. There was no close-by exit from the building there, so they knew they wouldn't be interrupted by dashing kids carrying heaps of children's books to their parents' cars out back. George always brought a small yellow pad to their meetings with a pencil purchased from his alma mater, New York University, 20 years earlier.

Giuseppe was better equipped – he carried a laptop that was connected to the library's wifi and several reference books. He also had a large yellow pad to write on and a ball-point pen that he had borrowed from the Bellagio in Las Vegas two years before.

Giuseppe opens the discussion with: "I brought with me some books that talk about the Children of Israel and their wanderings into the desert east of Egypt before they finally found the 'Promised Land, the land flowing with milk and honey.' They wandered around in the desert for thirty to forty years before Moses got the sign from God to invade the Holy Land, after all the Jews who had begun their trek from Egypt had passed away. Only Moses and Aaron were left from that original Jewish contingent of slaves, which was probably twenty thousand or so in number. They were divided into twelve tribes. Then Moses turned the Israeli forces into the battles to slay all the small bands of non-Jews in the small strip of land to the east of what is now called the Mediterranean Sea."

"Then Joshua fit the battle of Jericho, and the walls came a-tumbling down!" George added.

There was a pause; then George asked, "How come the Children of Israel stopped when they came to Jerusalem and set up camp for a thousand years there? Why didn't they keep going north?"

Giuseppe had to think about that question for a moment. He knew from the flicks that he had seen on PBS that the Holy Land was a principal route between the 'cradle of civilization' in central Africa and the slow movement of the Afrikaners north toward the Black Sea and the crossover into present-day Europe at Istanbul (Constantinople). This migration from Africa to Europe had gone on for over 40,000 years, so it was conceivable that some of the Jews could have packed up and gone north with the Afrikaners, especially the ones who had found the land near Jerusalem not really flowing with milk and honey.

"Maybe God told them to stop when they got to the Jerusalem area, and maybe they wanted to stick together," Giuseppe suggested. "I would have hated to be the first Jew to cross the Bosporus and set up housekeeping in Europe.

"But several hundred years later, there were Jews in every corner of Europe," George responded. "Maybe they were a whole lot more adventurous than we give them credit for."

"Maybe."

"Anyway," Giuseppe continued, "Joshua convinced the twelve tribes that it was time to stop trekking up and down the sands of the Holy Land and settle in around Jerusalem. They found a source of water to the east of Jerusalem, the Jordan River, which flowed out of the Sea of Galilee, south to the Dead Sea. They were also pretty good at digging deep cisterns that held water for the dry season. The Jews were always sharp traders, so they probably sold a lot of stuff to the Afrikaners who were continually passing through on their way north to the Bosporus.

"The Jews didn't want anybody but Jews to settle around Jerusalem, so they kept the 'foreigners' moving north all the time. It's the same sort of thing that the Mormons experienced when they claimed the land around the Great Salt Lake in Utah as their own. They welcomed all the travelers from the east; sold them food, water, and young oxen to pull their wagons; then sent them off across the Great American Desert to mine for gold in California or farm the new Oregon territory.

"When these Afrikaners made it across the Golden Horn and the Bosporus at the place that would be named 'Istanbul' or 'Constantinople,' they had a big choice to make," George suggested. "They could go west and south, avoiding the Alpine Mountains and entering present day Italy, which really *was* a land flowing with milk and honey. Or, they could go west and north, which would put them into the Croatian mountains and finally into France and Germany."

"And France and Germany were a whole lot colder than Italy," Giuseppe added. "So when you were standing there in Istanbul facing to the west, you had your choice: Go to Italy and melt in the sun, or go to France and Germany and freeze."

"I wonder if some of those people turned around and returned to Africa," George suggested.

"The thing that I wonder about is how come all the Afrikaners in Africa were black, and those same Afrikaners, when they arrived in Croatia, were muddy white?" Giuseppe asked.

"Write that question down, George," Giuseppe added, "and we'll get an answer next week."

Chapter Two

Alexander

W hen Giuseppe and George met at the library the following week, both of them had collected several books that they wanted to discuss. There was no answer to the question about why the Afrikaners were mostly Black and the people who settled Western Europe were mostly Caucasian. No one has ever addressed the question of where the Caucasians came from, but everyone agrees that they came from Africa. The transition from Black to Caucasian may have occurred slowly over a period of 40,000 years.

"There were all kinds of groups of civilizations that became predators as the years wore on because they kept seeing groups of people around them who seemed to be more prosperous than they were," Giuseppe posited. "So there were continuous organized wars between these groups of people. The Hellenists of Greece became the first truly European power.

"The Greeks were different from all other predators that the Middle East had seen before, because they brought with them teachers, city administrators, and farmers who knew how to get more food out of the existing land. But the Greeks were soon overrun by the Romans, who had more sophisticated warring skills than the Greeks did," Giuseppe stated. "Both the Greeks and the Romans dispelled the beliefs of the people living around the Mediterranean Sea that there were huge sea serpents and other terrible animals in the water who could devour a ship and its occupants. But bad weather continued to wreck small ships on the Mediterranean Sea. That is true today."

"I think we should mention Alexander the Great here," George said. "His father, Philip of Macedon, built up a huge army in the early 300s BC. Macedonia was the heart of the Greek empire at that time. After Philip was assassinated, Alexander took command of the Macedonian forces, marched through the Bosporus, and turned south to conquer most of the countries on the eastern and southern rim of the Mediterranean Sea. After he conquered Egypt, the Egyptians named their capitol city after him. He received a hero's welcome when he entered the capitol city. The Egyptians had a flourishing economy there in North Africa, and they didn't want Alexander to spoil it."

"Alexander had this fixation with 'oracles' in his life," Giuseppe added. "He believed that every major battle could be foretold by these religious oracles who could see the future. So while his army was looting and raping in Alexandria, Alexander traveled by horse to the northwest limit of Africa (Libya) to consult with an oracle. The oracle listened to Alexander, and then told him that he would lose any further battles if he turned east, past Assyria. This made Alexander so angry that the killed the oracle and turned back to the east. His staff found another oracle along the southern border of the Mediterranean Sea, and Alexander went there to consult with him about his future war plans. This second oracle had heard about the misfortunes of the first oracle, and he assured Alexander that victory would be his if he continued east to Iraq and Iran. That was what Alexander wanted to hear.

"Alexander attacked the kingdom of Darius of Persia (Iran), and killed Darius. Then he continued east to conquer India, but his troops revolted because they had been on the warpath for over ten years. Alexander was killed in battle near Babylon in 323 BC, and his kingdom dissolved after that.

"Meanwhile," Giuseppe continued, "The Roman Empire was beginning to feel its oats in Italy, and they took up after Alexander floundered. They perfected the left-hand and right-hand infantry, who were armed with gigantic spears, and easily subdued all the territory around (the Alpha Phalanx and the Sigma Phalanx).

"We will talk about the Romans next week."

Chapter Three

Rome

G iuseppe and George met at their usual place and time the following week. The subject was the Roman Empire, which lasted on and off from about 300 BC to about 1450 AD. That's a long time.

"The people who called themselves 'Romans' were completely under the domination of the Hellenist-Greek consortium from 600 to 300 BC, but that hold began to break apart after Alexander the Great died near Babylon in 323 BC," Giuseppe began. "The Greeks had some great ideas on how to run a country (or a group of countries), but they became obsessed with defending their newly won real estate around the Mediterranean Sea and lost interest in what we would call 'democratic' principles today. But they had enough time to create a complex series of gods that kept the world going around, and we know about those gods even today: Zeus, Apollo, Hercules, Odysseus, Achilles, Orpheus, and so on. As soon as it was obvious that the Hellenists were losing ground around the Mediterranean, the Romans moved in and took command of the countries that the Greeks had subjugated only a few hundred years earlier."

"Soon the Roman Empire extended all the way from Egypt and Libya to the south, Assyria to the east, France and England to the west, and Germany to the north," George added.

"Right in the middle of all this reorganization of the countries around the Mediterranean Sea, a man named Hannibal emerged from the city of Carthage (a city that is today a part of Tunis, on the southern coast of the Mediterranean Sea, in North Africa). Hannibal's father and his brothers began a long-term plan to invade Italy from the north to defeat the Romans, primarily because the Carthaginians did not have the ships to transport a large army to southern Italy. So they marched their army west to the Pillars of Hercules and passed into southern Spain (Iberia), using small ships. The Carthaginian army was armed with small North African elephants. They defeated the Spanish forces of southern Spain and proceeded east to southern France and the Alps.

"Hannibal's father and his older brothers were killed in battle with the Spaniards and the Gauls and Celts of France, but the Carthaginians soon refurbished their armies with men from these countries. With Hannibal as their leader, the Carthaginians marched into Italy through the Po River after climbing the Alps is 218 BC. Hannibal won many battles and lost many battles with the Romans between 218 and 203 BC, but the patience of the wealthy Carthaginians wore out and Hannibal's primary source of funding ran out. Hannibal was forced to leave the army in central Italy and return to Carthage to find resources to continue the war with Rome, but he was never successful. Instead, the Carthaginian government made peace with Rome, and Hannibal fled Tunis to seek other means of defeating the Romans. He spent the remainder of his life leading armies raised by the countries to the east of the Mediterranean Sea, all of whom hated the Romans and wanted to defeat them in battle. But in the end, the Romans were the only army still standing. Hannibal took poison in 181 BC to end his life."

"The Romans had a lot of trouble collecting taxes from these disparate groups, but the group that caused them the most trouble was the Jews in Jerusalem," Giuseppe put in. "Over an eleven hundred year period, the Jews were taken into captivity several times, and their predicament was clearly described in the Old Testament. The King who took most of the Jews to Babylon was Nebuchadnezzar.

And a thousand years later, the Romans were having similar problems with the Jews. By this time the twelve tribes of Israel had decreased to only two tribes that could be identified: the tribes of Joseph and Benjamin."

"And it was about this time, close to a decision by most Christian scholars, that the time scale would be completely reset, beginning with the year 'zero'. A new era had begun," George finished.

Chapter Four

Jesus of Nazareth

The land that Moses had brought the Children of Israel to had been their property for several thousand years when Jesus of Nazareth was born. They had suffered greatly at the hands of warring groups around them, but their unfailing faith in the 'one God' who would lead them past trouble every time never changed. They had collected some great myths about the one God who had lead them to triumph over their enemies over the centuries," Giuseppe began.

"Joshua fit the battle of Jericho, and the walls came a-tumbling down!" George exclaimed again.

"If you know any Jewish people personally," Giuseppe went on, "you know that they are hard-working protagonists who are willing to take on the world just like it is. They don't suffer from any delusions that the world is going to give them a break – they know that any 'breaks' they get must be fabricated by themselves."

There was a pause, then Giuseppe continued: "About this time a young man emerged from a village north of Jerusalem, close to the Jordan River, who was greatly distraught because he felt that the religious leaders in Jerusalem in charge of the Jewish faith were failing to meet the needs of the common people. So he went on a campaign to confront the Chief Priest and his cohorts in Jerusalem with his grievances.

"In the Jewish world of that time, a man became an acknowledged 'adult' when he reached the age of 30," Giuseppe explained. "He was expected to marry at that time, and his father, Joseph, found him a bride named Mary Magdalene. Jesus had preached at so many of the synagogues in the area north of Jerusalem, stating that the Chief Priest and his staff were thieves and robbers, so Jesus and his disciples remained primarily in the north county of Galilee when the Chief Priest came looking for him. Jesus remained close to the Sea of Galilee. Most of his followers, or Disciples, were fishermen. This was a wise decision, to remain some distance from the Chief Priest and his cohorts in Jerusalem.

"But Jesus could not remain in Galilee forever," Giuseppe continued. "He finally had to confront the Chief Priest with his complaints. He decided to make his move just prior to the annual feast days of the Passover, the celebration reminding the Jews that God had 'passed over' their houses in Egypt when they were slaves and inflicted the non-believers with the loss of their oldest son.

"In the days that followed," Giuseppe went on, the Chief Priest was so concerned about this man from Nazareth who had succeeded in putting him in an untenable situation politically that he schemed with his staff to kill him. The job of Chief Priest was not an elective position – rather, each candidate who wanted the job (when the old Chief Priest died) would bring money to the Roman King in Judea to 'buy' the job. The Chief Priest who won the contest simply agreed to pay the most money to the Roman King.

George now took over the story. "Jesus came to Jerusalem and was greeted by thousands of common people who were becoming more convinced every day that this young man was the 'Messiah,' the one who would lead them out of the tyranny of the Roman government. But they were disappointed because he did not speak of revolt or insurrection. Rather, he spoke about creating an environment with your fellow man where you could trust and serve the people around you. It was an entirely new message, one that few fellow Jews could understand."

"So the Chief Priest arranged for Jesus' arrest and asked the Roman court to find him guilty of some blatant offense that would cause him to be killed on the cross. But the Roman King was not convinced that this man, Jesus, had really done something grievous. So he offered to let Jesus go, but the crowd would not have it. The Roman king took the easy way out (as most politicians do) and ordered him to be killed."

"It is not clear what happened to the body of the young man after he was taken off the cross," Giuseppe spoke. "His body was placed in a sepulcher owned by a wealthy man who had responded to Jesus' words. Forty-eight hours later, the disciples and their families came to the sepulcher to take the body to a burial site, probably close to his home in Nazareth. But the body was gone.

"So in the coming months and years, there was a myth created that Jesus of Nazareth had risen from the dead and that he was present within the congregation of his believers, now called 'Christians.' There were reports of sightings of Jesus of Nazareth at many remote places throughout the Roman Empire. This was the biggest thing that had happened in the lives of the common people of Judea in centuries.

"The news traveled fast, but only in those circles that were willing to accept such an unprecedented story — a man had been raised from the grave!

"The Christians tried to remember everything that Jesus had ever said. What did he mean when he said that the Jewish temple would be destroyed and that he would rebuild it in three days? Was he referring to the Jewish temple, or to himself? There were many unanswered questions.

"Many Christians looked for the imminent return of Jesus from his home in the sky, yet Jesus did not return. As these people got older, they realized that they needed to write down the story of Jesus for future generations. But none of the disciples who were the closest to Jesus could read or write. What to do?

"Eventually a group of young Jews that may have heard Jesus speak from time to time came forward and offered to put the Disciples' stories onto paper. But the writings were not completed until the Disciples were very old. It was nearly fifty years after Jesus died that the first written manuscripts appeared.

"There was a man named Saul of Tarsus who had a religious experience with Jesus (or so he claims), and he became the chief spokesman for the new religion. He wrote to all the new churches that had been formed in the Holy Land and visited them frequently to answer their questions about the risen Christ. He stated clearly that he had never met Jesus before the crucifixion but that he had been confronted by the spirit of Jesus on the road to Damascus. His writings constitute over half of the scriptures in the New Testament.

"It seems unusual that a young man who had never spoken to a Gentile in his entire life was suddenly the center of focus of a new Gentile religion that began with the raising of a young man from the dead. Hard to believe; but many people did believe.

"At this point in time we are confronted with a new phenomenon that mankind had never witnessed before. We have a collection of writings by men who were single-purposed in their efforts to tell the story of Jesus, the Christ. That story continues to be told today, over two thousand years since his crucifixion. Remarkable."

"But what were the religionists going to do with this story?" George asked. "It was too big a story to confine it to the Jews in the world – the Gentiles had to hear the story also. It was time for some organized group to collect and disperse the story of Jesus."

"We will talk about that collection and dispersal next week," Giuseppe promised.

Chapter Five

Organizing the Faithful

Once the story of Jesus was out, it spread throughout Asia Minor and Europe like wildfire. The common people were perfectly happy to accept as fact that someone of lowly birth who resided in Nazareth was actually the Son of God, and that he had been crucified and risen three days later out of the grave to lead his brethren to new heights of glory. The wealthy Jews were contemptuous of this Jesus story, but the lowly born Jews were willing to discuss the matter.

The only Roman citizen that believed fully in Jesus was the man Saul of Tarsus (Paul), who was among the most highly trained religionists in the Jewish world. He was a bachelor, and apparently never married. He spent his entire adult life vis-

iting the fledgling Christian churches throughout Asia Minor, explaining his views on how the
new church should be organized and presenting a
unified message to the rest of the world. He was
apparently about the same age as Jesus, but had
never met him. The New Testament (in the book of
Acts) referred to his 'experience' with Jesus on the
road to Damascus, but Paul himself never wrote
about this happening.

People didn't live as long in those days as they
do today; few made it past the age of forty. But
Jesus' Disciples lived longer than most. By the year
60, though, they were all gone, having waited all
their lives to see Jesus one more time. But young
Jews who could both read and write sat down
with the Disciples and wrote their remembranc-
es on parchment. The Hebrew language was not
a good language to write these memoirs because
it included no verbs. Any reader of the sacred Old
Testament scrolls had to provide his own verbs as
he read the documents to a synagogue gathering.

But there were other languages widely written
and spoken in Asia Minor by the religionists and
the commoners – Aramaic, Greek, and Latin. All
three languages provided all the nouns, verbs, ad-
jectives, and adverbs needed to speak and write
precisely.

The collecting of books as candidates to appear
in a final story of Jesus was interrupted in the early
70s AD when the Romans decided that the Jews had

caused them too much trouble with their insurrections. The Roman army marched on Jerusalem and totally destroyed the Temple built by Solomon. A small contingent of Jews left Jerusalem when the Roman army enveloped the area, and they moved to the top of a huge mesa that they had pre-positioned as a final battleground against the Romans. The mesa was named Masada, and its history remains in all Jewish folklore. It is about 30 miles southeast of Jerusalem, overlooking the Dead Sea. The Romans built a 375-foot assault ramp and breached the mesa in 73 AD, only to find that all 700 Jews had taken poison rather than be forced into slavery.

Two Gentile groups – he Eastern Orthodox and the Roman Catholic churches – immediately recognized the value of the Old and New Testament scriptures, and there was a race to capture the best copies of all the New Testament writings known to be in existence, including the writings by Jesus' Disciples and Paul. Jesus apparently knew how to both read and write, but he left no documents behind when he died in Jerusalem. Both Aramaic and Greek versions of these 'books of the Bible' existed in Asia Minor, but both the Orthodox and the Roman Catholic churches tended to translate them into Latin, the language of the Roman Empire.

The Old Testament had long since been translated from the Hebrew to Aramaic, the language spoken by most people in Asia Minor, in the

Septuagint. The books of the New Testament remained in Greek until the Roman Catholic Church commissioned St. Jerome in 387 AD to translate the New Testament into Latin. During his lifetime, Jerome translated all of the New Testament and half of the Old Testament into Latin, which was completed by his fellow monks after his death. That version of the Bible, known as the Latin Vulgate, served as the baseline text for both the Eastern Orthodox and Roman Catholic churches for over a thousand years.

There were some unexplained experiences in Jesus' life, so the Christian churches began to fill in the gaps with myths. For example, both the Orthodox and Roman Catholic churches spoke of Mary Magdalene not as Jesus' wife but as a 'camp follower' who traveled with Jesus and his Disciples and prepared food for them. The myths intimated that she had at one time been a prostitute (whore) and that Jesus had forgiven her. Mary, Jesus' mother, was elevated in the Roman Catholic Church as one who had been impregnated by God himself to create Jesus. She was worshipped in much the same fashion as Jesus was worshipped, and the Catholic Church decreed that she had never faced death – she was taken bodily to meet her Lord.

No special provisions were made for Jesus' father, Joseph of Nazareth. Mary and Joseph had several more children after Jesus was born, and the families of these children remained in the area of Nazareth. The family asked for the body of Jesus after he died on the cross, and a wealthy man named Joseph of Arimathea apparently offered the use of his tomb to place Jesus' body in. The New Testament tells the story of Jesus' mother and wife going to the tomb and finding it open, with the large stone at the front of the tomb rolled away.

The Roman Catholic Church named Peter, one of the Disciples, as the first Pope, posthumously. They also named Jesus of Nazareth as the Son of God, again posthumously. A special order of management people emerged from the Roman Catholics, an order called the Jesuits. They were routinely put in charge of any projects that the Vatican sought to complete, and they served as the leaders of all Catholic colleges, universities, and churches. This is still true today.

The Eastern Orthodox headquarters had migrated to Constantinople, a town that didn't exist until the fourth century. But Constantinople, which got its name from the Roman Emperor Constantine, was the gateway between Europe and Asia, and it was an excellent place for their headquarters. The Roman Catholic Church had moved their headquarters from place to place, but decided that Rome was the best location in the third century. Apparently the term 'Roman Catholic Church' did not exist until the close of the third century, when one of the letters written to the Pope referred to the facility in Rome as the 'Home of the Holy Roman Catholic Church.'

The Vatican kept a presence in the southern French city of Avignon for several centuries, due in part to the fact that the city of Rome became extremely hot and humid in the summer. This location provided much better access to the thrones of Europe, which were the center of Catholic power in Europe. No King or Queen could be crowned in Europe without the expressed permission of the Vatican, and the common people were informed that God himself had ordained this person (King or Queen) as their new leader.

In 325 AD, Emperor Constantine of Rome (who had declared that Christianity was the official religion of Rome) convened the Council of Nicaea. Many issues were resolved, including a first cut at which books should be placed in the New Testament and which should not. All of the texts that purported to be worthy of inclusion in the New Testament were retained, and it is for this reason that the books that were 'caste out' at that time continued to be in existence when, for example, the Mormon Church decided to write its own Bible in the twentieth century.

The Orthodox Church never had a Pope, but they did have a leader who convened Orthodox conclaves from time to time. After the Council of Nicaea, the Roman Catholic Church was organized into groups of Catholics according to the country they lived in, providing positions for Bishops, Archbishops, and Cardinals.

The dogmas of the Orthodox and Roman Catholic churches began to separate from each other. However, the concept of a 'Purgatory' where Catholics would await a cleansing period before entering heaven did not appear in Roman Catholic literature until the twelfth century.

The Purgatory concept made a great deal of money for the Roman Catholic Church. For example, in 1516 AD Pope Leo X made it known that he would relieve any Catholic of multiple years of Purgatory (5000 years) if the person would donate to the church to build the rejuvenated St. Peter's Basilica. It was this act that jump-started the Protestant Revolution by Martin Luther in Europe.

Following the establishment of this chapter of information, George and Giuseppe were worn out, and they both went home.

Chapter Six

Muhammed and Islam

From the viewpoint of the Europeans, very little of interest had occurred in the lands of the Arabic Peninsula or India, China, Japan, Mongolia, and Australia for centuries. But by the end of the seventh century, there was a religious upheaval occurring around them that forced their attention. This upheaval was the introduction of Islam by the Prophet Muhammed.

Muhammed was in his early twenties when he went out into the deserts surrounding Mecca; several months later he returned with a plan to unite the non-Christian world around him with commonsense theology and a return to the worship of one God – not thousands of gods, which his neighbors persisted in. He enveloped all the myths of the

Jewish world (Moses, Abraham, Joshua, and even Jesus of Nazareth) and rolled them into one continuous history of the downtrodden of the world.

He even accepted the Christians' view of an afterlife – that good people would go to a place of reward for living a good life after their earthly death. The first few years after he returned from the desert were filled with battles to convince his countrymen that Allah was the only god and all the other gods were false. Before he died in 632 AD, he was able to convince a lot of people that he was right. And he left behind a well-written 'bible' named the 'Quran' or 'Koran' that told his countrymen how to live.

Unlike Jesus of Nazareth, who took no position on wars and battles between countries, Muhammed gave specific instructions to his followers on how to deal with the non-believers and heretics amongst them. These people should be purged by his believers and killed if necessary. Muhammed's instructions to taking human life to preserve a presence of peace would seem to be totally unrealistic, but the Christians can boast of no better plan for the future of this globe.

It is alarming that most of the major wars that have been initiated on this planet in the last hundred years were begun by God-fearing Christians who wanted to rid the world of bad people. Should the Christians be proud of what they have done?

Are Christians appointed by God to police the entire planet?

As Giuseppe states, "Is Islam the wave of the future? I think not. Is Christianity the wave of the future? I think not. These religions have hampered man's quest for survival, not enhanced it."

Chapter Seven

The Twelfth Century

This was the century in which two important dogmas emerged from the Roman Catholic Church. The first was the creation of an intermediate state for departed members. This state, known as Purgatory, was never considered by the church as a permanent location for lost souls – rather, it was a temporary state where the dead awaited a move to their final resting place in Heaven. After the official creation of Purgatory, there were endless sales of 'indulgences' to all Catholics willing to pay to aid the deceased members of their family. These indulgences involved both dead and living members of the family. For example, an indulgence could be as simple as asking for the prayers of the priests at a local church for a now-deceased member of your family, or they could be as complex as asking for an annulment of a wedding in the family. There was no provision in the Roman Catholic Church for a divorce between a Catholic man and a Catholic woman. Once married, they were married for life, unless some sort of indulgence could be agreed upon between the Church and the family.

For example, in the official Cromwell text about his life as an advisor to King Henry VIII, Cromwell purchases 1000 masses from the Catholic Church to be said at the local church to aid his deceased wife in her recent death and move her from Purgatory to Heaven.

The second dogma was a clarification of the right of the Roman Catholic Pope to 'excommunicate' any heretic from the ranks of the Catholic Church. This 'excommunication' was often threatened by the Papacy but seldom used. It was used primarily by the Vatican to keep the Kings and Queens of Europe and England 'in line', warning them of the grave consequences that they faced if they challenged the Vatican in important matters.

Chapter Eight

The Thirteenth Century

The thirteenth century was plagued with wars and rumors of wars across Europe and Asia. The Arabic groups who lived along the Tigris and Euphrates Rivers (the Babylonian empire) were overrun by the Mongolians from the east in the 1200s, led by Genghis Khan. The Mongols ran out of gas physically when they conquered the lands that comprise Syria, Iran, and Iraq today, and they liked the warmer climate of the Middle East. They intermarried and settled into new lives there. There were very few Mongols who considered back-tracking all the way to Mongolia and putting up with the extreme cold of the north Asian continent.

At this time, the city of Baghdad was the learning center of the world. In later centuries some of the most learned men in England came to Baghdad for extended periods to read about the mathematics and other sciences that were contained in the Baghdad archives. For example, Sir Isaac Newton (1642-1727), a famed mathematician in England, spent years in Baghdad reading (in Arabic) the thoughts of the earlier mathematicians. He is credited with formulating the basics for 'The Calculus,' but some historians argue that that particular science existed in Baghdad long before Newton got there.

The scene in Europe was relatively unchanged. European historians call the period from the Fifth to the Fifteenth Centuries the 'Dark Ages.' This thousand-year period showed very little change in how the countries in Europe were managed. The common man made little if any progress in his standard of living. For example, a commoner could be executed for killing a deer in the forest if he did not receive permission from the King's agents to do so.

Late in the thirteenth century, a new phenomenon occurred in Europe that could never be explained by the people living there at that time. Today's historians call the period from 1300 to 1850 the 'Little Ice Age'; both Europe and western Asia were inflicted with cold weather that changed the growing patterns of their trees, shrubs, flowers, fruits, and vegetables. Scientists today speak of changes in the warm currents of the Atlantic and Pacific Oceans as a primary cause of the unexpected European and North American cold, but other information such as sun spots may have contributed to the situation. For example, in the 1700s the huge glaciers of Switzerland began to form, and in 1780 the entire New York City harbor froze.

Chapter Nine

The Fifteenth Century:
The Inquisitions

King Ferdinand   Queen Isabella

This is the century that many Americans associate with an awakening to discover the 'new' world. Americans know that 'in 1492, Columbus sailed the ocean blue'. But there was also a lot happening in the old country, known as Spain, in the 1400s. As Columbus was attempting to procure funding for a voyage to the new world, many commoners in Spain were being inflicted with a religious exercise known as the Inquisition.

The Vatican had authorized several smaller Inquisitions in various places in Europe, like southern France and Italy (an 'Inquisition' is a cleansing exercise of the church, to eliminate hidden heretics). But the size and the bloodshed associated with the Spanish Inquisition are appalling. There were at least 5,000 Spaniards burned at the stake, and at least 300,000 Jews were expelled from the country; some report that the number could have been as large as 800,000.

The Inquisition was originally intended to ensure the orthodoxy of those non-Christians who had been converted (with or without duress) to Catholicism. Queen Isabella and King Ferdinand established the Inquisition to ensure that it was conducted according to their wishes. The persecution of the Jews began as early as 1390, but it wasn't until 1480 that the entire political system of repression reached its zenith.

The Inquisition included the capture and destruction of hundreds of thousands of books written in every European language. The Inquisitors were not paid by the Spanish government so they paid themselves by ransacking the homes of wealthy people and selling the loot on the open market. The records of the Inquisition, which was not officially canceled by the Spanish government until 1834, were originally retained in Madrid then transferred to the Vatican. Those records would have been long since destroyed had it not been for Napoleon, the Emperor of France, who invaded the Vatican in the nineteenth century and took all of the Inquisition records back to Paris. These records are on display in Paris today. For his activity in this matter, Napoleon was excommunicated by the Vatican.

The Chinese Invasion of Europe

Everything you will be reading here came from Gavin Menzies' two books, *1421* and *1434*. Gavin Menzies was a commander of a British submarine that roamed the Pacific and Atlantic Oceans for several years, and while he was going from mission to mission, he learned to read translations of some of the oldest Chinese texts still in existence. His two books explained that the Chinese, in the early part of the European Fifteenth Century built huge three-masted sailing ships that sailed as far west as India and Africa and as far east as the Pillars of Hercules between Spain and North Africa. These sailing ships were over 100 yards long, and the three masts were arranged such that the center mast was perpendicular to the ship's deck but the other two masts were angled to the left or right to catch more air and propel the ship faster. Everywhere the ships went, including South America, North America, Africa, Europe, and the remainder of Asia, they gave presents to the people they met. The usual present was chickens, which accounts for why chickens are now present everywhere in the world.

While one of these ships was visiting Italy, in the Mediterranean Sea, they gave copies of their maps that showed the presence of the Gulf of Mexico between North America and South America. Their maps showed that there was no way to get through to China via the Gulf of Mexico – it was a closed cul-de-sac. The Chinese attempted to return to China via a northern route, but were caught up in the polar ice and never got through. They concluded that the only way to return home was around the southern end of South America. These maps also showed that there was a strange stream of ocean water that flowed from the waters west of Portugal all the way to the first islands of the Gulf of Mexico (the island of Jamaica), and a ship traveling west from Europe could make much better time by getting into this stream.

The Chinese also showed the Italians copies of text that had been produced on their 'printing machine.' European history later reported that Guttenberg had invented the printing press in Germany several hundred years later, and that

Columbus had sailed to the lands west of Europe without the benefit of any maps (which is a lie).

Chapter Ten

The Sixteenth Century:
The Age of Enlightenment

The sixteenth century began with an explosion of the arts in Italy, led by the three greatest artists of that era: Leonardo Da Vinci, Michelangelo, and Raphael. Da Vinci was the oldest, born in 1452. Michelangelo followed in 1475, and Raphael was the youngest – 1483. Da Vinci died first, in 1519. Raphael followed in 1520, but Michelangelo lived to be 88, and died in 1564. Da Vinci painted two of the most famous paintings in the world, the Mona Lisa and the Last Supper. Raphael painted frescos for Catholic churches all over Europe. Michelangelo completed the statue of David for the Vatican and repainted the Sistine Chapel with hundreds of life-like figures that looked down on the people in the chapel.

All three artists had little quirks that the Church had to deal with. For example, the original statue of David showed the man totally naked, and his penis and gonads overwhelmed the statue. This was not acceptable to the Church. So another artist was hired to place some sort of loincloth over David's privates. A copy of this statue later made its way to Florence, and no such loincloth existed.

Da Vinci's problems lay in his insistence that the earth rotated around the sun, when all religionists knew that the sun rotated around the earth. Da Vinci published a retraction of his claim to the earth moving around the sun, and the Catholic Church let him live. His only child, a daughter, was sent to a Monastery close to his home in Florence, but he and his daughter were not allowed to communicate with each other for life. Da Vinci was 'imprisoned' at his home the rest of his life. The great astronomer Copernicus was not so fortunate; he was burned at the stake for his insistence that the earth rotated around the sun.

By the start of the sixteenth century, the wealthy people of Europe, western Asia, and northern Africa were pretty much content with their lot in life. The era of kings was flourishing. Russia and the southeastern countries of Europe (Romania, Croatia, the Czech Republic, etc.) had firmly made peace with the Eastern Orthodox Church, and the rest of Europe was tied to the Roman Catholic Church.

But the sixteenth century featured bloodshed not seen before (except, perhaps on the continent of Asia and the Mongols). At the same time that the countries of Europe (including Great Britain) were trying to make peace with one another, they were also trying to fight their neighbors. For example, the Kings of Great Britain crossed the English Channel every twenty-five years or so and fought the French over land in northern France that was in no way a part of British sovereignty. The land belonged to the French.

Spain was constantly at war with the Moors, who had crossed the Mediterranean Sea centuries ago and set up their own civilization in southern Spain, in cities like Alhambra. But they were not Christians – they were of the Islamic faith. Trouble, trouble, trouble.

In 1215 AD, King John of England had signed the Magna Carta, a document drawn up by the Archbishop of Canterbury to bring peace among the warring factions in southern and northern England. But by the sixteenth century, the guarantees of representation of the common man amongst the House of Lords and the House of Commons had ceased to exist. Some of the delegates to the House of Commons were actually elected by their constituencies, but most were merely appointed by the warlords who controlled the land, like the Duke of Norfolk or the Duke of Sussex. What appeared to be a working parliamentary procedure was a façade.

What about the religious rights of the common man during this time? At the beginning of the sixteenth century, the Archbishops, Bishops, Monks, and Prelates of the Roman Catholic Church controlled nearly one-third of the useable farmland in Britain. Martin Luther, Zwingli, and Calvin had not yet come upon the scene. The Crusades to the Holy Land had finally died out, but at a horrible cost of men, animals, equipment, and money. All the kings of Europe were broke.

The common people of Europe were caught in the strong grip of the Roman Catholic Church, which sold indulgences and millions of special masses to move the relatives of wealthy departed souls toward a better relationship with Heaven (out of Purgatory).

Then in 1517, Luther posted his famous '95 theses' on the main entry door of the Catholic Church in Wittenberg, Germany, All bets were off. He had to flee for his life and lived at the home of a wealthy German in Prussia for a time, and then finally returned to Wittenberg when it was clear that the Catholic Church could not come into town and burn him at the stake.

But others were not so fortunate. William Tyndale, a British scholar, began writing an English version of the New Testament, and he was immediately pursued by the armed forces of Henry VIII to stop this effort. He escaped England and lived in Antwerp, but was captured in 1536 and was returned to England, strangled, and then burnt at the stake. At that time, several thousand copies of his English Bible had been smuggled into England, despite the efforts of Sir Thomas More, who called Tyndale a heretic. Under More, the price for being caught with a Tyndale Bible in one's possession was immediate strangulation. (Why this man is called "A Man For All Seasons" is a never-ending source off wonderment.)

Thomas More (later named a saint in the Roman Catholic Church) was later charged with treason by Henry VIII and beheaded in 1535.

Just 75 years after Tyndale's death, King James of England ordered that an English version of the Bible be created and offered to the public (1611).

King Henry VIII is the man who chose to break with the Roman Catholic Church after the church would not grant him a divorce from Catherine of Aragon (after 22 years of marriage) so he could marry Anne Boleyn . He set up his own church, The Church of England, and made the Archbishop of Canterbury the administrative leader of the church; there was no such thing as a Pope. Later Henry VIII named himself as the leader of his church.

The only living child that Henry VIII had with Catherine of Aragon was Mary, who was declared later to be illegitimate. She spent most of her life in Scotland; hence her popular name, Mary, Queen of Scots. As soon as the British legislature approved Henry VIII's break with the Vatican, he divorced Catherine and married Ann Boleyn. Ann Boleyn presented Henry with a child soon thereafter, a girl who was named Elizabeth.

After Henry had Ann Boleyn beheaded for treason, he married Jane Seymour. Jane gave Henry a son who was named Edward VI. Edward VI was too young to reign over England when Henry VIII died in 1547 (being only ten years old), so the kingdom was governed by a board lead by his grandfather. Jane Seymour died only three months after the birth of Edward, and Edward himself died six years after his coronation. Elizabeth became the Queen of England in 1553 and served in that capacity for over fifty years. Among her first duties as the new Queen, she had Mary, Queen of Scots (her older half-sister) brought to London and beheaded for treason.

He subjects called her by many good names: Good Queen Bess and The Virgin Queen. She never married.

All of Europe and Western Asia were coming out of the Dark Ages by the start of the seventeenth century. The people were hampered by unusually cold weather, which would persist for another 200 years. This was the time when the huge glaciers of Switzerland began to form; now in the twenty-first century, they are melting away.

Elizabeth of England died in 1604 and was followed by King James I. He had been the first king to be raised as a Protestant; she was the last of the Tudor Kings/Queens. King James is best remembered for his instructions to the Archbishop of Canterbury to produce an English-language Bible that all his subjects could read. This may seem like a simple matter, but there were powerful forces in England that wanted to keep the Bible in Latin (The Vulgate), so the only persons who could read the Bible were the Clergy. Recall that William Tyndale had been strangled and burnt at the stake by order of Sir Thomas More only 65 years earlier.

Science began to claim a larger share of the newspaper stories carried in each city's dailies in Europe. A scientific revolution was led in England by Sir Isaac Newton (1642 – 1727) and Francesco Mario Pagano (1748 -1799). Some called this period the Age of Reason. Bertrand Russell spoke of the Enlightenment as a 'phase in a progressive development, which began in antiquity.' Russell argued that the Enlightenment was ultimately born out of the Protestant reaction against the Catholic counter-reformation.

In France the Enlightenment became associated with anti-government and anti-Catholic church radicalism, while in Germany it reached deep into the middle classes, where it expressed a spiritualistic and nationalistic tone. Neither

German government nor church government was threatened. Lutheranism had become the country's state religion. In Italy, Spain, and Russia, the Enlightenment showed itself as a flourish in the arts, and in England the Enlightenment released a spasm of scientific activity. There was little or no movement in the Scandinavian countries, primarily because they were so far advanced in aspects of political socialism, and downplayed the interaction of religion with secular government.

South and Central American nations were becoming bigger players on the world stage, but the Catholic Church had reached them earlier (with no competition from the Protestants). All the governments and schooling systems of South and Central America mimicked the formulation of these supposedly secular activities in Italy. But these countries had no Kings and Queens.

The swap-out of Kings and Queens in Europe and western Asia continued unabated for another 200 years, with each generation of non-elected political leaders losing some small part of their autonomy with the advent of each new generation. There was no 'divine right of Kings' discussed in these countries anymore, nor were the Kings and Queens allowed access to the country's treasury.

The common man wanted an elected President and a Legislature responsible for creating laws. Some of the more thinking commoners wanted relief from the seemingly arbitrariness of the court system as well, something that we continue to hope for today.

Chapter Eleven

The Eighteenth Century: American and French Revolutions

The eighteenth century came on with a flurry of activity in France. The long succession of Kings Louis after Louis continued unabated. But a great race was on between Spain, England, and France to capture large parcels of land in the New World. Spain had entered North, Central, and South America from the wide open Gulf of Mexico; they claimed all of South and Central America plus 70 percent of the land in North America. The English could claim only small portions of the eastern edge of North America and a few small islands in the Caribbean. The French had come into the New World via its northern route, and claimed the 'cold belt' of land along the northern edge of the continent (Canada).

As time passed, it became evident that Spain could hold all of South and Central America because the other world powers were not interested in these lands. The southern part of the North American continent (Mexico) was also undisputed. The Spaniards had searched both Central and South American for the existence of the 'cities of gold' and the 'fountain of youth,' and found (to their dismay) that all these myths were false. But the Spaniards had reached the Pacific Ocean from the confines of their claimed territory in the new land, and the world was beginning to understand just how large this new land really was.

It had occurred to all three countries that one way to gobble up large parcels of new land in the Americas was to defeat the other European countries who claimed those lands. Hence, the main feature of the eighteenth century was one unending war between France, Spain, and England to dislodge these territorial claims from the European claimants. Spain had a distinct advantage in these activities because it had found silver in the northwestern reaches of South America (and some gold also) on the Pacific side of Central America. Even today there is no good estimate of how many Indians living in South America were collected up, enslaved, and sent into the silver and gold miness to die.

England made the decision early in this contest not to attack Spain at the source of its silver and gold, but to wait until these metals had been loaded on slow-moving ships in the Caribbean and attack them once they had left the safety of the new land and were approaching the open sea of the Atlantic Ocean. England made its base of operations in the island of Jamaica, the last island these silver-laden ships would pass before they arrived at the Portuguese Azores. The British pirates were careful never to sink a Spanish vessel – they would simply destroy all its inhabitants and tow the ship into a Jamaican port after they attacked the ship.

In the stories about one of Jamaica's Governors, a man named 'Black Beard,' had at one time 70 Spanish ships for sail in the Jamaica ports. Their original names had been removed from the ships, and the governor would put whatever name you wanted on a ship once you bought it.

The Americans in Boston and New York also participated in these pirate activities. They would form up a pirate team from local unemployed sailors in Boston or New York and sail south, supposedly to buy rum and bring it back to the American east coast. They would attack Spanish ships that no longer had a Spanish Man-O-War escort, kill everyone, move the heavy metals to their pirate ship, and sail the Spanish ship to Jamaica to sell it. When the hurricane season began, they would cease operations, pick up rum in Jamaica, and sail home to Boston or New York. The Spanish were never able to shut down the British and American pirating operations in the Caribbean.

Very late in the eighteenth century, when it became obvious that England and the English-American Colonies were going to clash over taxation and property-owning issues, the French King Louis immediately made his naval armada available to the Americans. He also sent a renowned army leader, Major General Lafayette, to aid General Washington in training his troops for the forthcoming wars with the British. History has never explained why Louis decided to spend so much time and money to defend the American claims to autonomy, except to say that he hated the British enough to ensure their defeat anywhere in the world.

At that time (the 1770s), the King of England, King George III, was in a particularly bad financial situation. He hadn't won a clear-cut war against the French or Spanish in years and years. The colonies were costing him a lot of money to maintain, and other than tobacco, there was no agricultural product that could raise his revenues significantly. The silver and gold out of the Caribbean had pretty well dried up, also.

What to do? What to do? He did the only thing he could do: Send a small, relatively untrained British army to the colonies to teach them a les-

son about how the King of England should be re-
spected. But why a small army? Because the King
of England was saving his big army to take on the
French. France had been kicked around by all the
counties of Europe for generations, and most of
the time the French entered a war, they ended up
paying the other side money to shut the whole
thing down and go home. But the French were no
longer the patsies that they had been one hundred
years before.

Most Americans think that the American
Revolution occurred rather quickly – beginning
in 1775 and ending three or four years later. Such
is not the case. The British forces under Burgoyne
surrendered in New Jersey in 1777, and the official
peace treaty was signed in Paris in 1783.

The French Revolution broke out soon after the
American War for Independence ended. There is
no question but that the support of the French in
the American Revolution was the deciding factor
in the American victory. This revolutionary spirit had been brewing in France for several generations, and it was unstoppable when the peasants marched on the national prison, the Bastille,
in 1789. The result was violent bloodshed; King
Louis XVI was beheaded, as was his wife, Marie
Antoinette, and his only son. There would never
be a French monarchy again, or so the commoners
thought.

The commoners and newspapers made Marie Antoinette appear as a force in the neglect of the French government toward their economic problems, but in fact she had nothing to do with the economic dilemma France found itself in. She had been taken from her home in Austria when she was thirteen, fabulously outfitted to meet her new husband (who was 15 at the time), and could not interest him in the immediate problem of creating a male heir for the French throne. All he was interested in was hunting.

Marie went on some shopping binges in downtown Paris with some of her wealthy French lady friends, and the newspapers called her a traitor to the economic pinch the nation was feeling. So she made a deal with her husband to bring him to her bed, and father three children, while she discontinued her visits to the great shopping centers of Paris. From her viewpoint, that was what Queens were supposed to do: provide a male heir and spend money to support the local economy. She did both.

One reason that the French Revolution dragged on for so many years was the greed of the European nations that encircled France. When Louis XVI was beheaded, the British smelled possible success in northern France and attempted to gain territory there. The Germans marched into northeastern France with the intent of occupying all of France, but they were stopped far short of Paris and Versailles. Meanwhile, the Spanish, who had remained quietly in Europe after their Armada was sunk, suddenly decided to claim French land north of the Apennines. It took the French several years to chase the British back to England, the Germans back to their borders behind the Ruhr and the Rhine River, and the Spanish over the mountains.

The French were also hampered by the changing attitudes of their National Assembly, a large group made up of the landed gentry, the churchmen, and representatives sent to Versailles from all the provinces in France. The first thing that the National Assembly did was to take away the lands and structures that had been owned by the Catholic Church for hundreds of years and sell them to rejuvenate the broken French treasury. Louis XVI was an extremely devout Catholic, and he fought vigorously to keep the Assembly from taking over the Church's lands, all for naught.

Next, the Assembly ruled that any peasant who had lived on a patch of land for more than X years would become the owner – with no payment to the landed gentry. The landed gentry responded with furious challenges to the authority of the National Assembly, and the Assembly wrote some new laws that required the peasants to pay the noblemen for their patch of land. This was land that had been deeded to the gentry by the Kings of France and the Popes – it was free. Now the gentry wanted significant remuneration for their losses. Unfortunately, the amount of money that a peasant would have to pay to the gentry under the new laws was more money than they could raise in one hundred years, so that plan floundered also.

There would have never been a final settlement of this issue except for the fact that the British, Germans, and Spaniards were all knocking on the doors of France, and the Assembly had to do something to unify their people and run the foreigners out of the country. The peasants finally had to pay some monies, but nothing close to what the landed gentry had demanded.

Once the full bloody impact of the French Revolution was known all over Europe, the other monarchies in Europe and western Asia quietly waited in their castles and winter homes for the return of Constitutional Monarchyism throughout the continent. Removing themselves from the limelight worked to perfection: Twenty years later, most of the lessons of the French Revolution had been forgotten, except that France was never able to keep a monarchy for any length of time again and several other European nations were forced to declare themselves as republics or democracies. It was unclear what these new terms meant to the commoner in Europe, but it sounded like a good idea.

The notions of the 'divine right of kings', the 'special privileges of the wealthy', and the 'preferred treatment of the Clergy' were all gone now – tossed into the scrap barrel along with any thoughts of revisiting the medieval periods of the European and Western Asia continents. But why did the bloodshed in France *not* boil over into England, Spain, the Low Countries, Germany, Austria, and Russia? There are a lot of different reasons. In England the huge landowners like the Duke of Norfolk and the Duke of Sussex had maintained large standing armies, mostly to keep the English kings in check, whereas the French landowners had long since abandoned their personal armies and given the defense of France to the king. When the commoners revolted in France, there was no standing army at the huge landowners' fortresses to stop the pillage.

Spain had a whole set of problems of its own, caused primarily by the efforts of the Spanish kings and queens to defeat all inroads by Islam in the southern part of their country. In addition, the communications between France and Spain were so poor that the Spanish never realized what was going on in Paris. The Lowland Countries had already made their move to initiate a constitutional monarchy form of government, as had the Scandinavian countries. Germany and Austria made their moves toward a constitutional monarchy at this time, but the counties of southeast Europe did nothing. Russia did nothing.

After all the bloodshed, a man named Napoleon Bonaparte picked up the pieces of the French nation, made himself the Emperor, and proceeded to take on the rest of Europe. Napoleon kicked ass all over Europe, including the sacred group of Roman Catholics known as the 'Vatican,' which he ran off and took a lot of their treasures back to Paris. But Napoleon made the huge mistake of taking on Russia; not because they were such a formidable foe, but because their capitol, St. Petersburg, was thousands of miles away. After taking a severe beating from the Russians during one of the worst winters in European history, Napoleon returned to Western Europe, where his armies were soundly beaten by the European conglomerate lead by the British Duke of Wellington at Waterloo, Belgium. End of Napoleon.

But the King of England had long since lost his war in the American colonies, and the Americans were ready to kick his butt in the years to come. However, the British returned to America in 1812 and ran all of the federal bureaucracy out of Washington, D.C. The only maneuver that saved the fledgling republic was a series of peace talks where the Americans paid a lot of money to recompense King George III for his losses in the Revolutionary War. It was a lot easier to pay money than to fight another war.

Chapter Twelve

The Nineteenth Century: The Industrial Revolution

Having brushed aside the multi-thousand year claims of the monarchies, the very wealthy, and the clerics, it remained for the republics and democracies of this world to create a new order. This was difficult because the world's population had never been in this situation before. For thousands of years, someone had always told the common man what to do, and he did it. At this point in time, this common man had to make some decisions for himself.

All over the world, people fully expected the American experiment to fail under its own weight from bureaucracy and indecision. But it didn't happen. How could any country operate without a king? The Americans borrowed a lot of ideas from their British counterparts, who had been laboring with a Magna Carta government for over 700 years. There would be no House of Lords, but there would be a U. S. Senate. There was no House of Commons, but a House of Representatives. There was no king – only a president. And all these people would be elected to their offices, not appointed.

The writing of the United States Constitution suffered through a lot of special interests in Philadelphia, and in the main those special interests lost. Some of the important issues confronting the new government were never addressed in the Constitutional Congress – the best example being what to do with the notion of slavery in America. The answer to that question would have to wait a hundred years to be answered.

Unfortunately, a lot of people who came to America thought that the notion of taxes had been left behind in the old country. Not so. America could not function without a sizeable tax base that provided basic services to its people. The issue of what constitutes good and bad tax policy is still with us today.

In the last twenty years of the eighteenth century, there was world-wide excitement about creating a manufacturing base within most of the countries of the world. Europe took the lead and America followed. The Americans elected a new president almost every eight years, but the common man in America depended on the legislative branch of government (the Senate and the House) to provide the continuity needed for long-term planning.

In England, one particular monarch, Queen Victoria, served as the titular head of the government from 1837 to 1901, reigning almost two years longer than King George III. She had very little political power during this period, but she was an advocate of the bully pulpit that made U. S. Presidents like Theodore Roosevelt so popular. Her nine children married into royal and noble families across Europe, earning her the title of Grandmother of Europe.

There were thousands of inventions during this period, but the one that was the cornerstone of this period was the steam engine, invented by James Watt in England. His engine provided power for all the manufacturing facilities across the world and later for all the mobile devices like trains and cars. The heat source was wood, which was the most plentiful fuel on the earth. Soon coal, which had become popular for home heating, replaced a lot of the wood-burning steam engines because coal burned much hotter than wood and provided greater heat for a given amount of fuel. The invention of the liquid-fired internal combustion engine had to await the invention of oil-based fuels (gasoline).

The inventions of commercial electrical lighting, electrical signage, radios, phonographs, and home-lighting all occurred during the lifetime of one man, Thomas Edison (of General Electric – the Wizard of Menlo Park, NJ) (1847 – 1931). America became the undisputed master of new ideas – many of them stolen from Europe and Japan.

Chapter Thirteen

The Twentieth Century: Wars and Rumors of Wars

Unfortunately, with the inrush of the industrial revolution, there also occurred a return by the nations of the world to the savagery that had characterized the fifteenth through the eighteenth centuries. Early in the twentieth century, the entire world was talking about the unstoppable forces of major war between the countries of Europe, and the expected war broke out in 1914 when a visiting archduke from Austria was assassinated in Serbia. Within a month the lines had been drawn: Britain, France, and Russia as the Allies, and Germany, Austro-Hungary, and the Ottoman Empire as the Axis. Soon, Italy joined the Axis. The Germans invaded the neutral countries of Belgium and

Luxembourg to encircle the French, and a Western Front soon materialized on the ground, separating the Allies and the Axis armies. This Western Front would remain virtually unmoved until 1917, when the Americans joined the Allies.

In Eastern Europe, the Russians enjoyed great success against the Austro-Hungarians, but German forces intervened to stop the Russian advance in late 1914. For three years, the war in the east and the west continued with no signs of abating. In March 1917, the Russian government collapsed when the Bolsheviks overran the home country and the Czar and his family were killed. The Bolsheviks immediately sued for peace with the Axis to give them time to form a new government in Russia.

The American government (particularly the Congress) had refused to interfere with the war in Europe, and President Woodrow Wilson narrowly won re-election in 1916 on the campaign slogan "He kept us out of war." Shortly after his re-election, he proposed an American entry into the war to save the Allies. He sent General John J. Pershing to England with the American Expeditionary Force in 1917. He raised taxes to pay for the war and passed the first draft of young American men to fight the war. He loaned billions of dollars to England and France and sold the first Liberty Bonds to pay for the loans.

As soon as the momentum swung to the Allies to end the war, German Chancellor Ludendorff sued for peace. His armies had destroyed Belgium, Luxembourg, the Netherlands, and parts of France, but he did not want the same destruction to occur in Germany. The Germans signed a peace treaty with the Allies in a railroad boxcar in the Compiegne forest in November 1918.

When the war ended in 1918, Wilson began a campaign to form a League of Nations to keep the world from re-entering world war, but the American Congress defeated his plan. Was there any sanity involved in the process that the world had gone through? On one hand there were the Germans (faithful Lutherans), the Austrians (faithful Catholics), and the Italians (faithful Catholics), who were killing and maiming the British (faithful Church of England), the French (faithful Catholics), and the Soviets (faithful Eastern Orthodox) on a daily basis. What would cause these two groups to do this? The answer lies in the commodity that we all really worship: money. If you have lots of money, you are happy; if you have no money, you are not happy and you are willing to go out and kill for money. So let's not proclaim our allegiances to the religions of this world and frankly admit that we don't really give a damn what they do.

But the established religions in this world have a trump card that they play on a daily basis. That trump card is a statement that religion controls your future in the next world (your life after death), and you had better give them plenty of attention, else they will send you to Hell.

Do the wealthy people of this world pay attention to their religions? You bet they do. They will heap money upon every religious idea that a priest, archbishop, cardinal, or pope presents to them, with the guaranteed return from the church that this new money will make them a better candidate for Heaven someday. Imagine their thought processes. Are you going to stop making these outlandish contributions to a church that has never made good on any of its promises? Hell no. You have so much invested in glorifying the church that you dare not stop now and endanger any position you have with the holy men above (St. Peter, etc.) What to do? What to do? Just keep giving them more money and hope for the best.

Between 1918 and 1933, the world attempted to enjoy some level of peace. In America there were overtures to allow voting rights for women (women's suffrage, 1920) and the removal of beverage alcohol from our daily lives (Prohibition, 1920). Women's suffrage endured, and Prohibition did not.

Americans wanted to forget about war, and any efforts by the Presidents and the Congress to maintain a fighting force were soon abandoned. There were more important things to think about, like the completion of the Panama Canal and the opening of trade agreements between the USA and both the eastern (European) and western (Asian) nations. From the American point of view, the 1920s were a time of great 'release' from the horrors of war and a time to think about 'cruising down the river on a Sunday afternoon' or how 'you are my sunshine, my only sunshine.' Americans had to contend with Prohibition during these years, but that too would pass eventually.

During this period between the World Wars, the capitalist ideal grew significantly, and the world became smaller with the advent of railroads and airplanes. Charles Lindbergh became world famous for his flight from New Jersey to Paris in a single-engine aircraft named *The Spirit of St. Louis*. He married Ann Morrow, and they had a child in 1930. The child was kidnapped in 1932, and he died shortly after he was taken from his family. The kidnapper was executed. Charles died in 1974, and shortly thereafter it was revealed that he had fostered seven children by three women in Europe. Ann died in 2001 in America.

In 1929, the Great Depression began. The stock market collapsed, and as a result, most of America's major industries collapsed too. This Depression spread worldwide. There were a lot of people to blame for this financial meltdown, but they all folded themselves into the background in America and let a President and a Congress sort it all out. America's politicians pondered and

Americans waited for a day of recovery. A new, young President named Franklin Delano Roosevelt (FDR) stepped into the breach and tried to lift America up by its bootstraps, but improvements in the nation's economy came slowly.

Then, in 1941, the Japanese bombed Pearl Harbor in Hawaii, and America's politicians had a reason to go to war. This war would lift us out of depression and recession and start us off on a path to economic prosperity that had never been experienced before in any part of the world. The only price the Americans had to pay was the loss of the lives of millions of young men and women who were killed in action and buried in Europe and Asia. For every person who died, there were five or six significantly wounded who returned to the USA and then lost their way in the flurry of after-war activities. There were returning alcoholics and drug junkies; people who lost arms and legs and eyes and ears; people who were gassed; people who lost all their confidence to return to a non-war life – the people who were damaged on the inside. We Americans didn't understand these kinds of maladies – hell, buck up kid, and get back to work because the war is over! Don't you understand? It's time to be happy again.

Such was not the case in Europe and Western Asia, unfortunately. No sooner had the First World War ended than several countries began working on the Second World War. Three nations in Europe would become battlegrounds again: Spain, Italy, and Germany. The Communists in Russia had firmly established their position on two continents, and it was time for the rest of us to be 'afraid.'

Troubles began in Italy in 1933 when an aggressive political party named the Fascists began to take charge of the northern parts of the country, under the leadership of Benito Mussolini (El Duce). The same thing happened in Germany in 1933 after Adolph Hitler was named their Chancellor. But there were significant differences between the evolution of 'warrior states' in Germany and in Italy. Both men (Hitler and Mussolini) used the existing legislative system in their country to gain voting seats in government. Hitler moved quickly to dominate the German people and their economy (and their religion) with harsh new rules; Mussolini moved much more slowly to win over the Italian people and their economy. But he used their religion to eliminate any competition during those years.

The Roman Catholic Church had settled its headquarters in Rome, and Mussolini established his headquarters a couple of miles away, on the other side of the Tiber River. The Pope, who was the leader of the Roman Catholic world at that time, was Pius XI. Mussolini and Pius XI made a long series of agreements between them (mostly secret) to control all facets of life in Italy from 1933 to 1938. Mussolini wanted the blessing of the

Catholic Church to perform his political functions in Italy, and Pope XI wanted the government to rid the country of all its non-Catholic influences – including non-Catholic schools, Protestants, and Jews.

They were a great team for a while, and then differences between the Catholics (who considered themselves to be the only true Christian religion) and the Fascists (who were religious in name only) began to drive them apart. Strangely enough, Pius XI considered the Communists to be a worldwide threat to his Church (the Communists had crushed the Eastern Orthodox Church in Russia), but he failed to view the German Third Reich as a similar foe. Then, as Hitler began to bring Catholic priests and nuns into the German courts in 1942 and '43 to charge them with pedophile-type crimes, Pius realized that the Third Reich was not his friend. Pius XI died in 1939, and his successor, Pius XII, attempted to mend the breach between the ruling parties in Italy and Hitler in Germany. But by this time World War II had broken out, and the true intentions of Adolph Hitler – to annihilate all the Jews in Europe – became evident.

The Roman Catholic Church was careful never to speak disparagingly about the Holocaust, and the Germans were careful never to destroy the real estate or attack the employees of the Roman Catholic Church. Many churches were destroyed in World War II, but few of them were Catholic churches. There is a great book on the newsstands now: *The Pope and Mussolini*, by David Kertzer, that explains in detail all the machinations between the Popes Pius XI and XII, Mussolini, and Hitler. You owe it to yourself to read this book.

The Spanish Civil War got started in 1938, just two decades after World War I ceased. There were loyalist forces that supported the Spanish monarchy (the Republicans), and revolutionary forces and Communist forces lead by Francisco Franco (the Nationalists). Franco finally won in 1939. This is the war reported by Hemingway's great novel, *For Whom the Bell Tolls*.

Adolph Hitler became the Chancellor of Germany in 1933, and, despite the agreements that Germany had made to end the Great War of 1918, Germany began to re-arm to take on its foes in Europe. In 1938 and 1939, Germany seized Czechoslovakia and Austria, and in 1939 they invaded Poland. At that point the entire European war was unleashed.

The same team that had taken on Germany in 1914 was called to stop the Germans again: Britain, France, and the Soviet Union. The Scandinavian countries moved toward neutrality in the coming war, as did the other smaller countries of Europe. Finland declared its neutrality reluctantly, based on the fact that its unending battles in the Great War and its constant defense of the border with

Russia had cost that country more than half of its young men.

Once again, Italy sided with the Axis forces of Germany, and then switched allegiances in 1943. Romania and Poland stood with the Allies, while most of southeastern Europe attempted to remain neutral. These attempts at neutrality were not unusual, given that southeastern Europe had faced unending war, pestilence, and famine for the previous 300 years, as one large nation after another marched into their farmlands from the north and took away their livelihoods.

So the stage was set for yet another European war, only two decades after the defeat of the Germans in 1918. As America had done in 1914, it again attempted to isolate itself from the problems of Europe. The American Congress was unified in its demands that America 'stay out of another European war.' But the President of the United States, Franklin Delano Roosevelt, was so concerned about the possible defeat of the Allies in Europe that he initiated a program called the Lend Lease program that gave war materiel to Britain, France, and the Soviet Union. He sent them money to finance their war effort, sold war bonds, and told the American people that this money would be returned someday.

The only way to get this war materiel to England in the 1940s was by ship, so the American merchant marine was revitalized to perform this task. But the German navy was one step ahead of America – they had a large submarine fleet that destroyed hundreds of cargo ships as they made their way from America to Europe. The President couldn't really discuss this situation with the American people because they were too involved in having a good time and finding sources of illicit booze. But the bodies of the merchant marines continued to bob up along the Atlantic Coast.

About this time, a nation that Americans considered an outlier (Japan) had some ideas of its own on how to conquer their part of the world. Quietly, the Japanese collected their war materiel and prepared to invade several of the Pacific islands. They avoided Australia because it was too big. They had already conquered and settled into most of the heavily populated regions of China with very little effort, since the Chinese Army was controlled by an unremarkable general named Chiang Kai-shek. This man was the last of a long line of Chinese warlords who controlled the people of China with an iron fist.

China was never able to rid itself of the Japanese until 1945, when America dropped atomic bombs on Hiroshima and Nagasaki. But by this time the Communist Party of China, led by Mao Tse-tung, had infiltrated most of China, and Chiang Kai-shek and his forces were forced to retreat to the island of Taiwan. The Chinese Nationalists were never able to mount a serious attack against the forces of Mao Tse-tung.

The war against the Germans ended formally on May 8, 1945, and the war against the Japanese ended formally on August 19, 1945. This war cost between 50 and 85 million people their lives, including the 6 million Jews involved in the Holocaust.

Chapter Fourteen

The Second Half of the
Twentieth Century

This text could go on for pages and pages describing all the wars that America participated in between 1945 and 2010. But why bother? Have we become a nation of warmongers, who like to destroy other civilizations around us? I think not.

Then what is our problem? From time to time, America is compared with the earlier great nations that rose and fell over the centuries. There were the Greeks (the Hellenists), who brought education to the nations they defeated, a law system that was pretty good for its time, a language that outdoes anything invented since, and history and philosophy that have survived the centuries. But where is Greece today? Can the Greeks claim world leadership in any venue today? I think not. Why not? I would suggest that the wars that Greece fought for several centuries finally sapped its people of the energy to continue to be a great nation.

What about the Romans? Did the Romans demonize their subjects any more than the Hellenists did? I think not. Why are the Romans gone? I think I know the answer: they fought war after war after war, and finally found themselves incapable of continuing to survive in the world and its money-based economy.

Who is next? England? America has always been a step or two behind England in its pursuits of excellence. I swear that the English legal system beats our system all to pieces because we Americans have allowed judges and lawyers to take possession of the entire legal process. Do you remember the O. J. Simpson trial of a few years ago? Some attorney (either for the state or for the defense) would drone on for several minutes, supposedly asking a question. Then the only thing the witness on the stand could say was *Yes* or *No*. Why couldn't the judge simply ask the witness to tell the court what he or she knew about this case? Why are our courts so concerned about 'legal correctness' that they stifle the words of the witness on the stand?

If Americans are not warmongers, why do we participate in so many wars? The answer is simple: There are many wealthy people in America who make greater fortunes when this nation is at war than they ever do if we are a time of peace. By constantly stirring the war pot, there are wealthy Americans who are guaranteed vast profits in the future.

These wealthy people must be very careful not to get their children and grandchildren actively involved in these wars, however. If they did, these children would be killed on the field of battle, and this defeats the purpose of constant warmongering. The wealthy want to manage a war, not participate in it. So the next time a President of the United States comes onto the TV during prime time and explains to us commoners that it is essential that we go to war someplace (as young George Bush did when he invited all Americans to go to Iraq and die), then you should turn the TV off. What this President is really saying is that the economy is stagnating and the only way he or she knows to boost it up is with a war. To some in America, war is a means to stimulate the economy.

Was this true in World War II? Well, of course. Unemployment completely vanished after FDR gathered all Americans and got them to work together to defeat the German Axis. Was FDR being a hypocrite? Was all that he really wanted full employment in the United States? No, I don't think so. He was sincere in his fear of what the German Third Reich was trying to do in Europe.

What about the Vietnam War? Oh, please, spare me! The people who genned-up the Vietnam War were bureaucrats who wanted to fight someone somewhere to show that Communism was going to lose! Remember all the discussions about the 'domino effect'? According to the domino people, if we (the USA) did not intervene in Vietnam, the Catholics would suffer terribly in Indochina. So when an Archbishop visited the President at the White House and told him that the Catholics in Vietnam were being horribly mistreated by a man named Ho Chi Minh, the warmongers stepped up to the TV cameras and proclaimed our duty to fight for Vietnam!

How bad of a man was Ho Chi Minh? Was he a despot, another Adolph Hitler or a Joseph Stalin? The answer is *no*. He was a Vietnamese patriot who wanted the French and the Americans to get the hell out of his country. But the French wanted to remain in Vietnam because the rubber plantations there were making vast monies for the wealthy of France. And the Americans wanted to remain in Vietnam to show the world how tough we really were.

Do you remember how the Vietnam War ended? Were there any ticker-tape parades on Manhattan Island when the men came back from Vietnam? Who exactly won this war?

Did we, the Americans, learn our lessons from Vietnam? Hell, no. As soon as young George Bush could arrange it, he mounted a campaign to send American troops into Iraq and defeat that terrible person, Saddam Hussein. Was Saddam Hussein a terrible person? The answer is *yes*. Was it worth the lives of several thousand of our GIs to root him out of Iraq? Hell, no. Did the President's staff have to lie a lot to get America involved in the Iraq War? *Yes*. Who was the biggest liar? We all know that – his name was Dick Cheney, Vice President at that time, and he is the biggest political liar of all time. But he did a great job for his corporation, Halliburton, and they made tons of money from the Iraq War. He also set up a situation where private security had to be provided for the many bureaucrats who visited Iraq all those years, and the owner of that private security firm is now a billionaire several times over.

How many more wars do we, as a nation, plan to participate in over the coming years? Is there a way to stimulate the economy and a way to reduce unemployment without choosing war? Aren't the lives of our young men and women worth more than that?

Will Americans ever stop participating in war when the President makes the clarion call? I doubt it. Part of the problem is that young people consider themselves to be immune to disaster. How do we know this? Well, how many young people will die in automobile accidents this week because they refuse to hook up their shoulder belts when they get in a car? Other people may die in accidents, but not me! According to these young people, only old people die.

Chapter Fifteen

The Twenty-First Century

"We have made it to the twenty-first century," George announced. "How nice to be here!"

"We still have a lot of unanswered issues before us," Giuseppe remarked. "But the world has made some progress in the last two thousand years."

Giuseppe continued with: "I think that church financing is a whole lot like running a political campaign at this point in time. The people who need money to do what they do are gracious enough to accept the smallest gift, but they would much rather accept a very large gift that would pay their bills for a long time. Take the Roman Catholic Church, for example. In the last thousand years, they have been able to sell something to their parishioners that raised significant funds, either to build new facilities or pay their monthly bills. Centuries ago this saleable item was indulgences, and because of this, Martin Luther rose to fame and notoriety when he challenged the Catholic Church on the indulgences issue. Today no one can sell indulgences, but the Catholic Church can still sell an item worth just as much – the promise to conduct special masses for the dead in your family and move them closer to Heaven from their present position in Purgatory.

Take, for example, the Kennedys of Massachusetts. They are a proud Catholic family that makes a lot of money in liquor, theaters, movie film distribution, and the stock market. When the last of the famous four brothers (Joe Jr., John, Robert, and Ted) had passed away, the Kennedy family heaped millions of dollars on the Catholic Church to get their boys into heaven. These were great men, men who served America throughout their lives. Joe Jr. died in World War II, John and Robert were politicians who were both assassinated, and Teddy died of natural causes after serving in the U. S. Senate for an eternity. But the only way they could make it into heaven was to pay the Church to pray for them and move them along towards their final resting place. So the Kennedy family will continue to pay the Catholic Church millions of dollars every year to ensure the safety of all the Kennedy clan in the afterworld, including all the wives involved and the younger generation of Kennedys.

What an incredible travesty the Church has imposed on the Kennedy family! Perhaps the Kennedy family feels that this is money well spent; but how can they really know? Are they simply feathering the nests of a lot of religious bigwigs who enjoy the high life?

Once you begin paying these exorbitant fees, you can never stop. If you ever stop paying, will your deceased in the family have to settle for residing in Purgatory forever?

There was a pause. "Do you feel confident enough to make a few predictions about what is going to happen in the future?" George asked.

Giuseppe had to think about this question. A lot of the pivot points in human history hinged on events that seemed to be totally irrelevant at the time, but turned out to be extremely significant later. Giuseppe thought to himself, "If that Archduke had not been assassinated in Serbia a hundred years ago, would the world have been thrown into World War I?" He knew that the answer was probably *yes* because some other minor event would have lit the fires for that war. If people want to fight, they don't need much of an excuse.

"What if Adolph Hitler had never been born?" Giuseppe asked himself. There again, if not Hitler, it could have been some other screwball that wanted to fight the world.

There was a pause.

"I am waiting for your predictions," George reminded him.

OK, it was time to speak:

Number one: The power of professional religionists has been deteriorating all over the globe for several thousand years. There are good reasons for this deterioration. Religionists offer a lot to the commoners (like peace of mind, safety of the family, a social system that gives following generations a place to meet and socialize, and finally, a guarantee of some kind of eternal life if the commoner follows the rules of the church.) The problem with this arrangement is simply this: The professional religionists have failed to ever deliver on their promises. It is easy to offer eternal life to the masses because no one has ever come back from the portals of death and verified the claims of the church. So we, the commoners, simply have to take the word of the church on this matter. If a member of your family experiences great tribulation (like physical or mental illness) then the church lays the blame for that tribulation on your family, and charges you with dereliction of duty. The church certainly cannot be blamed for these faults in the master social system. Don't blame God or Jesus Christ – blame yourself. If you blame God, then you are obviously a heretic!

People are living longer, and they are living smarter. More and more people around the world are understanding that the claims of professional religionists are empty promises. God will not provide eternal life for you, he will not ensure that your family will never become financially destitute, and he will not guarantee that you will live without serious disease and medical problems as you grow older. The God whom you worship has no control over these issues. As a result, the only churches that will survive the next two hundred years are those that offer significant social outlets for family members, and the worship of God or Jesus Christ will become a secondary issue. Churches will become the twentieth century equivalent of the Grange, the organization that offered social activities to the farmers in America a hundred years ago.

Number two: All the professional religionists are discovering that the world no longer desires to pay for religious excesses – their awesome churches, their beautiful private homes and winter retreats, their vast collections of art, their unending pomp and circumstance. The next time you see a large gathering of the common people at the Vatican, cheering for the Pope, ask yourself, "Why are these people here?" Is it because they love the Pope so much? Maybe. Is it because they have nothing at home that even begins to compare with the wealth and splendor of the Catholic Church? Yes, now you have hit on the reason for their coming to the event. If they have given a few nickels to the church, then they can claim that in some small way, they made all of this possible.

But fewer and fewer people are willing to donate monies to the churches, and the religionists are actively seeking alternate means of financial support for the coming centuries. What would these alternate means consist of? The Roman Catholic Church claims about 1.2 billion members, almost 25 percent of the people who inhabit the earth. These people have been squeezed for money for the past two thousand years, and they are no longer responding to calls for greater gifts to the church.

But there is one alternate source of money that has not been claimed by the churches, and it is the banks of the world. Some banks make money and some do not. But the ones that do not have only themselves to blame because the money sources in the world have not dried up. It is true that many of the little banks that have gone into bankruptcy or sold out to the bigger banks did so because they could not compete in the current banking world. The little banks had to become more efficient in money-handling or get out of the business.

The churches of this world, and particularly the Roman Catholic churches, have gone after the banking industry because banks are a never-ending source of revenue. Those banks may not be making money today, but they are destined to become money-makers in the future! But who are the competitors in this world who seek to own the banks, rather than the Catholics? They are the Jews of this world, and they are just as smart as the Catholics (and maybe even smarter).

These two groups play by different sets of rules, however. The Jews pay the prevailing price for all their assets, and they are willing to pay the bank CEOs exorbitant fees to keep a bank running. But the Catholics are not. After all, they have a ready corps of financial advisors (named the Jesuits) who are willing to run the biggest banks in the world for peanuts in remuneration. Why offer a Jesuit millions of dollars in salary when the church can offer him eternal life with all the 'perks' of office at the right-hand of God? So the battle is on, and in a couple of hundred years, we will know who the winner is. In any bank auction, the Church will outbid all others to gain the bank, then slowly bleed it to bring its operating costs down to make it profitable. In their view, time is always on their side.

Number three: In the next 200 years, the exorbitant art wealth of the Vatican will be distributed around the world to enhance the appeal of the Roman Catholic Church everywhere.

Number four: In 200 years, the Eastern Orthodox Church will have ceased to be. The reasons for their demise are simple: They refuse to buy into the big money-makers invented by the Roman Catholic Church (like Purgatory and Indulgences), and the lack of funding from these sources is driving them bankrupt. There are some other churches that will go bankrupt also, or they will consolidate with churches that have similar beliefs, but these consolidations are only a temporary means to avoid their eventual demise. Strangely enough, some of the more dogmatic churches, such as the Southern Baptist Convention, are the most in danger of folding since they have alienated the affections of the majority of Protestants. The Catholics have hated them for centuries. Both the Catholic Church and the Protestant Churches will be replaced by Pseudo-Protestant Churches that offer dazzling weekend entertainment to their parishioners and care for the children and the aged. They will continue to hold worship services, but those services will be attended for reasons other than worship.

Number five: The Mormon Church already reached its zenith (as has the Southern Baptist Church). The Mormon Church suffers from dark decisions made early in its history and the acknowledgment that their original leader, Joseph Smith, was in fact an oversexed shyster and a thief. The claims of tablets of gold and Smith's supposed creation of the Mormon bible are ridiculous beyond belief.

Number six: The creation of Islam by the prophet Muhammed was a necessary intervention into Middle East history to provide a reasonable counter to the claims of the Catholic Church in the early centuries. Without Islam, a vast number of people in the Middle East are left without any hope for eventual equality with the Europeans and Asians. The presence of the Jewish nation in the Middle East will continue to be a thorn in the side of most Muslims. But the Jews in America, who contribute vast sums of money to both the Democrats and the Republicans, are unwilling to disassociate themselves from the Nation of Israel, even though they despise some of the antics of Israel's present leaders (who seek to control the Middle East with their 8 percent of the population and keep a harsh fist on the 92 percent who are Arabic).

Those in America who seek a close relationship with Israel, at the expense of the Palestinians, are willing to ignore the present inequities in the Holy Land, suggesting that there is something prophetic about the situation there, which has been ordained by God. They will tell you that the Arabs will always be the servants of the Israelis. They are very wrong, of course. To quote the Kingston Trio of thirty years ago, "Someone will set the spark off, and we will all be blown away!" When the Nation of Israel ceases to be, there will be a mass exodus of Jews from the Holy Land back to the USA. They will be received into this country with great trepidation and fear because most Americans have not yet learned to live quietly with a large Jewish population. But where else can the Jews go?

This is the same trepidation and fear that most Americans show toward the present day Muslims who have immigrated to this nation and set up their own circles of society. It has taken a couple hundred years for the Italians and the Irish and the Blacks to intermingle with the vast numbers of white, Anglo-Saxon Protestants and Catholics who like to call America 'their country.' We are all immigrants, but we like to forget that. The Muslim immigrants who have formed their enclaves in the bigger cities in America (where they can find work) are proceeding through the same stages that every other group of immigrants has experienced. They will take the jobs in America that no one else will take, and they will make do with whatever salary they receive. Their day is coming in the future, though, and they know it. But the price they will pay to advance in the worker-corps of this nation will take away any religious uniqueness that they now hold. Their girls will cast off the foolish clothing about their faces (the burqa or hijab) and they will intermarry with men of all faiths and beliefs. They will give up some part of their present religion for the guarantee of a good life in America in the future.

Number seven: The Islamic faith will continue to grow, but Christianity (including both the Catholics and the Protestants) will slowly ebb over the next 200 years. The religions of the Pacific Rim will continue to grow slowly in America, but not at a rate that alarms the Caucasians of this country.

It is ridiculous to say that Islam will grow in the

Middle East because most of the people there are already Muslims. Their problem is that the various sects of Islam can't seem to make peace with one another, and the result is constant warfare in that part of the world. Most of the remainder of the world has mixtures of all faiths, all creeds, and all colors, and the people seem to know how to live with one another in relative peace. But not in the Middle East!

What is the secret of their continuing discontent? We all know, of course. It is their religion that keeps them apart. It is their religion that causes one group of Muslims to build bombs and deliver them to another group of Muslims while they are worshipping their God at a mosque. Muslims kill each other, constantly. I don't think that Muhammed had this kind of duplicity in mind when he created the Quran (Koran) fifteen hundred years ago. He knew there would be differences among the readers of his text, and he knew that there would be significant bloodshed to take away the precepts of the Arabs toward multiple gods (sometimes hundreds of gods, much like the god worship in China several thousand years ago).

Today the Islamic world is split into several groups that do not speak to one another: The Sunnis (75 to 90 percent), the Shiites (10 to 20 percent), the Wasabis (3 percent), etc. The Wasabis claim to be the most conservative (and orthodox) group, and they are supported by the King of Saudi

Arabia (where the oil is). The only countries that are predominantly Shiite are Iraq and Iran. The Sunnis dominate Syria and Western Iraq. The current group of plunderers in the Middle East known as ISIS (Islamic State of Iraq and ash-Sham) are predominantly Sunni Muslims. The Wasabis will disappear when the oil disappears in the Arabian Peninsula.

The lesson to be learned from all this is: Don't live in a country that mixes its religion with its politics. No country can withstand the terror of a political system that mixes in its religious beliefs with its governmental beliefs and grants to some religious leader the ability to veto everything the government wants to do. This sort of religious hegemony existed in the Catholic Church (both Eastern Orthodox and Roman Catholic) in the Dark Ages when a Pope could supposedly veto any rule passed by a monarch or a legislature. All of that ambiguity finally went away by the tenth century, and no Pope ever attempted to override any monarch or legislature after that. But that is exactly the situation that is occurring in the Middle East right now. And there will be no peace among the various groups of the Islamic faithful until all the religious leaders of the Sunni, Shia, and Wasabi groups pass away.

There was a time, fifty years ago, when the world thought that most of the oil reserves in the world were in Saudi Arabia. But we know now that is not

AN OCCULT HISTORY OF THE RIGHT SIDE OF THE GLOBE

true. If you are less than twenty years old when you read this text, you will probably live to see the oil in Saudi Arabia disappear completely, and the world will turn to some other source of energy to transport stuff around the world. Good luck. When this occurs, the Saudis hope that they will own most of the shipping facilities around the world and that these facilities will support their people on the Arabian Peninsula. While the Roman Catholic Church concentrates on owning banks, the Saudis are concentrating on owning shipping facilities.

Number eight: The Spanish speakers of North America: The immigration quotas set by the American Congress have never been fair to many ethnic groups in the world. For example, the Asians have always been granted minimal immigration access into America while the Europeans have an open, unending access. There is no limit on Canadians who want to live in the USA. But there are severe limits on the Spanish-speakers who live south of the USA, in Mexico, Central America, and South America. For some reason, the US Congress fears massive immigration of people from the south. So many of the Spanish speakers have taken the problem into their own hands and they come to America in the dark of night.

As most of us know, these are the people who perform our most odious tasks in this country. The women cook our food, diaper our babies, and clean our bathrooms. They take the children for walks around the block, fix their clothing when it tears, and buy the groceries at the local grocery store. The men build our houses and commercial facilities, lay the brick and paint our walls, and install our roofs. So why do Americans hate these people so much? Could it be that the American people are afraid that if labor becomes too plentiful and too cheap here in America that they (the people who got here first) are going to suffer financially when wages and salaries are set? I have never been able to figure out this miasma of personal feeling among the whites of America toward the Spanish-speaking minority.

There was a pause. "Are you finished?" George asked.

"Yes, I am through," was Giuseppe's reply.

"You look very tired."

They agreed to meet the following Thursday.

"What are we going to talk about?" George asked.

"Money," was the reply. "Money, the root of all evil."

Chapter Sixteen

Money, Money, Money

On the way over to the library, George had stopped at the ATM and taken $200 out of his bank account. When he and Giuseppe sat down in the library, he put the ten twenty-dollar bills on the table. "The root of all evil," George said.

"But we can't live without money," Giuseppe suggested. "Sure, there are credit cards and there are bank checks, but simple cash is the way most of us do business."

"For now," George suggested. "Who knows what we will be carrying around in our billfolds twenty years from now?"

A pause, and then Giuseppe continued: "I have been thinking about money, and I read in the paper where some family here in town gave a pot-full of money to the performing arts league so they could continue presenting Broadway productions, etc., in this town. The paper didn't say how much money the family gave to the league, but it is probably a lot."

Giuseppe continued with, "Suppose that some really wealthy person, like 'The Donald', for example, decided that he was going to give some church more money than they ever saw in years and years. Suppose he approached the Vatican and told them that he would give them 200 million dollars if they would use it to build a new basilica in St. Louis, Missouri."

"Why St. Louis?" George asked.

"Because they need one," Giuseppe replied. "Now I'm not saying that this really happened – this is just a hypothetical case. But The Donald is known for giving money to lots of groups just to do things like this. He's a good man – he is a funny man. Suppose he offered the Vatican 200 million dollars to begin the building of a new basilica in St. Louis?"

"So?" George asked.

"What would the Vatican do?" Giuseppe asked. "We know that the Holy See himself would not enter into any discussion with The Donald, but he has staff at the Vatican who handle financial matters like this. How would the staff respond?"

"I have no idea," George responded.

"Here is what I think would happen," Giuseppe answered. "After a month or two, the Vatican staff would reply to The Donald's offer and tell him that they have a good use for the 200 million dollars, but not to build a new basilica in St. Louis. They would make a counter proposal: Build a small, $125 million basilica in St. Louis and build a $75 million dollar basilica in Karachi, Pakistan, because the Catholics in Pakistan really need a new building for worship. They would argue that a 200 million dollar basilica in St. Louis would be larger than St. Peter's Basilica in Rome, and that would be an insult to St. Peter. No Catholic would ever be allowed to build a basilica larger than the one at the Vatican."

"So St. Peter would be angry?" George asked.

"Absolutely," Giuseppe answered.

"So how does this story end?" George asked.

"I don't know," Giuseppe replied. "I assume that The Donald would meet with his financial analysts somewhere on Manhattan Island and try to come up with a better compromise."

"What we have here is two parties that never compromise on anything – the Roman Catholic Church and The Donald," Giuseppe continued. "They would be at a stalemate."

"When you come up with the answer about how these two parties would settle this question, will you tell me?" George asked.

"Absolutely," Giuseppe responded. "But remember that this is just a hypothetical case."

Giuseppe continued: "I think I am going to

have get on the telephone and call the Vatican and make some sort of a deal with them myself. I will propose to begin a new fund called the 'Move Donald Trump from Purgatory to Heaven' fund. I will pledge $10 a month to the fund to ensure that The Donald is moved swiftly to Heaven."

"But Donald Trump is not a Catholic," George announced. "Maybe he is a Lutheran."

"Then I will call the Lutheran Church in America and ask them to start a 'Move Donald Trump from Purgatory to Heaven' account to which I will contribute $10 a month."

"The Lutherans don't believe in Purgatory," George reminded Giuseppe.

Giuseppe was now confused.

"Why would you do all this?" George asked.

Giuseppe answered immediately. "Because so many people are always telling Donald Trump to 'go to Hell,' and that is not fair. If the Lutherans only have Heaven and Hell, then I need to ask them to set up an account to move The Donald from one place to the other."

"What if he goes to Heaven?" George asked.

"Then I have wasted my money," Giuseppe explained. "Better be safe than sorry."

"I will try to find the telephone number of the Lutheran Church in America for you, so you can make that call," George said.

Giuseppe resumed. "My family lived in Deutschland for several years after the Second

War, in Munich, Dachau, and Mainz. During all that time I do not remember a single utterance from the Catholic Church in Bavaria nor the Lutheran Church in the rest of Germany that tried to apologize to the Jewish people of Europe for all the horrors that the German people had inflicted on them. All the religious groups were so anxious to save their own skins that they were pleased to offer the Jews to Hitler to assuage his anger. If Hitler had run out of Jews to kill, then he would probably have turned to the Catholics and the Lutherans to keep the Holocaust going. Hitler had long ago learned to divide and conquer his enemies."

"Have you become a staunch atheist at this time?" George asked Giuseppe.

Giuseppe had to think about this question. He began with: "My wife asks me this same ques-

tion all the time. I think that she agrees with me on most issues, but she is slow to condemn the churches of this world for the dilemma we find ourselves in. She points out that the churches teach a moral code that is basically correct – that mankind should learn to care for the people around them and not run over them roughshod. The teachings attributed to Jesus of Nazareth are good teachings – he never tried to solve the political problems of his country. He dealt with life on a much closer venue – your next-door neighbor."

Giuseppe continued: "I would take issue with

those inside the church who claim that the church is the sole repository of true morality. I can be a moral person but not a church person. I can be a moral person but not believe in Jesus of Nazareth as the Savior of the World."

"But you can't have it both ways," George interrupted. "Either you believe in him or you don't."

"Not true," Giuseppe responded. "I can simply say that I am undecided about the claims of the Christian Church, just like I am undecided about the claims of the Islamic Church or the Hindus of India or the Buddhists of the Pacific Rim. There is no doubt in my mind that Muhammed, when he wrote the Koran, included all the great figures of former religions as Prophets of Islam to ensure that he made no one angry. He also offered his readers the right to eternal life because the Christian

Church had already included this piece of dogma in their religion. He didn't want the Muslims to be second-class citizens."

"Are we finished?" George asked.

"I am very tired," Giuseppe replied. "The only remaining text that I need to write is a short explanation and apology to the three young women in my life (my daughters) who have known me for fifty years. This text is a bit of a divergence from the face I have shown to them since they were born. I don't want them to think of me as a traitor."

There was a pause, and then George asked, "How

come you never want to talk about all the events that have gone on in the last two thousand years in the Pacific Rim countries?

"George," came the reply, "it is not that I don't want to talk about the Asians. It's just that I don't *know* anything about the Asians. How can I say anything about all the great things that went on in China and Japan and Korea and Australia and thousands of islands in that part of the world, when I don't know anything about them?"

"Next time we do this," George suggested, "Let's find ourselves an expert on the Pacific Rim."

"Agreed!"

"I know of one such expert, but he is extremely busy these days."

"What is his name?" Giuseppe asked.

"Gavin Menzies," was the answer. "He has written two books, *1421* and *1434*. He's a Brit, and he sailed under the Pacific and Atlantic Seas in a UK submarine. I guess he had a lot of time on his hands while his U-boat was patrolling the oceans of the world. You should read his books. Many European historians are going to have to rewrite their histories now that Menzies has revealed what was going on in the eastern half of the globe for several centuries."

Another pause. Then George stated, "I guess I didn't realize when we started this series of meetings that you were such a hard-over atheist, Giuseppe."

Giuseppe replied immediately. "I am not 'hard-over' on anything, George. But I know that in the beginning, man created god in his own image, and began from that day forward to charge the un-known god with all the bad things that happened in that man's life."

In the beginning, man created god.

In the beginning, after the big bang, the skies were forming up, and we happened to appear on an insignificant rock that looked like a cue ball in that explosion. Four billion years later, we appeared as creatures who had come out of the ocean. end of story.

"We will look at the entire text next week."

Chapter Seventeen

An Apology to my Daughters

As I sit here alone, I think about the many years my family spent together (my wife, Pat; our three daughters, Lisa, Annalori, and Jill; and me) cavorting over the world as an Air Force team. During those years we spent a lot of time in Protestant churches, attending worship services and classes and social events. Those were wonderful times. If I had a dollar for every church service I attended over those years I would probably be a wealthy man. I learned how to teach Sunday School and how to pray at open meetings. I became a Deacon and I visited lots of people who were home-bound and took the elements of Communion to them.

My wife never said a word to me about doubting any of the beliefs of our church. We had both grown up in conservative southern churches where the Bible was supreme, and we knew that the Gospel was meant to be spread all over the face of the earth.

Then one day, long after all the kids had spread their wings and flown away, I realized that I really didn't believe all the things I had said over the past forty years. I confessed to my wife the doubts that had arisen in my religious experience, and she told me that she also had the same doubts about our religious life and Jesus Christ and all that. We were still soul-partners after all those years.

You do not 'unJesus' yourself in a short period of time. Rather, you talk with yourself a lot and try to decide what is best for yourself, your spouse, and your children in the months and years to come. When the grandchildren come, then there are family events that occur fairly frequently. At one end of the line there were our parents' funerals, and at the other end the acceptance of the kids into church, followed by weddings. In all these cases, silence seemed to be the best approach. When we visited our families in Central Florida and North Georgia, there was a lot of joy expressed at our coming, and every event began with a prayer to Jesus Christ. Every meal was preceded by prayer also. We (Pat and I) didn't do those things at our house any more. We attended their churches in silence.

At what point do you tell your families in the Bible belt that you no longer believe all that bull-shit about Jesus of Nazareth and all the wonderful things he has done for the people of the earth in the last two thousand years? One of my neighbors staunchly credits Jesus of Nazareth with the defeat of the German Axis in 1944 – we could never have done it without him. He chose us as the victors and made the Germans the losers. Oh, spare me!

But these same people who will credit Jesus of Nazareth with all the successes that America has experienced in the last 200 years are very careful *never* to charge Jesus with misconduct in the fam-ines and floods and disasters that have occurred in our country over the years. According to them, if you were ever to mutter a complaint against Jesus, he might hear you and send you directly to Hell some day! You never know.

My neighbor has also explained to me that he has a lot invested in the Christian Church (he is 80 years old) and he isn't about to 'change hors-es in the middle of the stream' and say something unkind about Jesus of Nazareth. If he does, the golden bookkeeper in the sky may quash his case. "Richard," he says to me, "you are sounding more and more every day like a god-damned 'atheist', and that scares me."

AN APOLOGY TO MY DAUGHTERS

To which I answer, "Harold, I probably am an atheist. If you don't believe in Jesus of Nazareth, why bother to believe in a God? Being an atheist isn't all that bad." Harold knows better than to attempt to march me through all the claims of the New Testament because we have been through that many times before. "Jesus raised a man from the dead!" Harold exclaims. I correct his statement: "No, Harold, the Bible *says* that Jesus raised a man from the dead; but the Bible may be wrong."

Now there is anger in Harold's eyes. "Then you don't believe that the Bible is the infallible word of God?" he asks. "That's right," I reply. "The Bible makes lots of mistakes. What about the reference in the Bible about Jesus' casting devils out of people and sending those devils into a group of swine nearby? Then the swine charge into the sea and kill themselves. Do you believe all that, Harold?"

No, Harold didn't believe that. The score is now 'one' for the atheists and 'zero' for the Christians. "Then you don't believe that Jesus rose from the dead and proceeded to the right hand of God?" Harold asked. "Right," I reply. "I do not believe that. When Jesus' body was taken down from the cross, it was put temporarily in a tomb built by Joseph of Arimathea for himself, and later the family returned his body to Nazareth for burial."

"Then why have archeologists never found Jesus' body in Nazareth?" Harold asked. "Because the archeologists don't know which body to search for," I replied. "We don't have Jesus' DNA on file, you know." My religious discussions with Harold always end in a total standoff. We can agree on the future of the Denver Broncos football team, but not on theology.

"But what if you are wrong?" Harold says. "What if you find out when you die that Jesus really is the Son of God?" "I'll take my chances," I reply.

Well, daughters, that is my final message. I am going to take my chances and not try to repair any relationship that I have had in the past with the Christian Church. Any attempt at re-establishing my credibility with the Christian Church is fool-hardy, from my viewpoint. For two thousand years, the Christian churches have lied to us, and they will continue to lie because they have so much to lose if they admit their mistakes. My choice may not be your choice, of course. You may choose to continue in the church and raise the next genera-tion of children any way you like. You can tell the grandchildren and the great-grandchildren that their great-grandfather was simply a loony, and that will be okay. Come to think about it, you don't have to tell them anything about me. Just show them a photograph or two of an old man who lived long ago in a tiny house on the Colorado prairie with his adorable wife, and let it go at that.

* 9 7 8 1 9 3 8 7 5 7 3 2 7 *